T0167813

BE MORE KEANU

BE MORE
KEANU

JAMES KING

◙ SQUARE PEG

CONTENTS

—

Introduction 6

—

—

INTRODUCTION

We all need to #bemorekeanu.

Authenticity. Freedom. No BS. In a
film industry not known for any of
those things, Keanu is a truth-seeking,
bike-riding, kind-hearted (yet still ass-
whooping) breath of fresh air. He's an
innovator, an instigator and a long-haired
lover. A guru on a surfboard. A rock 'n'
roll philosopher. 'All we are is dust in the
wind, dude' his Ted Logan tells us in *Bill
& Ted's Excellent Adventure*. The guy's like
a sexy Yoda.

'All we are is dust in the wind, dude.'

TED LOGAN, *BILL & TED'S EXCELLENT ADVENTURE*

As Bill and Ted's friend Socrates (or indeed *So-craytes*) himself once said, 'wisdom begins with wonder' – and that makes Keanu Reeves our most triumphant mentor. Mixing martial arts with melancholy, butt-kicking with Buddhism, Keanu is an actor who follows his own script and a seeker who follows his own path; equal parts idol and vagabond, the ultimate badass bohemian searching for sense and serenity. He's wonder-*full*.

It's there in his private life, today's middle-aged Keanu continuing to do the same thing he's always done when not in the spotlight: climbing onto his 1973 Norton Commando motorbike and riding the roads of California, looking for answers; part petrolhead, part pilgrim.

It's there in his films: *John Wick*, *The Matrix*, *Little Buddha* (where naturally he plays *the actual Buddha*) and even in *Bill & Ted's Excellent Adventure*, a story entirely about the joy of experience and open-mindedness, rather than tediously memorising dates from a textbook. Whether it's through surfing or suffering, philosophy or a phone box, Keanu's always learning something. Plus, in turn, teaching us things too.

And it's in that famously blank expression – a face as stony as a Michelangelo yet also really *absorbed* in the moment, especially when mechanically delivering dialogue. It's a focus that shows diligence and industry. Someone painstakingly dealing with ideas and ideologies. Someone honest.

Yet there's always been something otherworldly about Keanu too. His background is diverse (born in Beirut to a British mother and Chinese/Hawaiian father, then raised in Toronto), his personal life unusually sad (the loss of family and friends is well documented).

—

'When you truly understand karma then you realise you are responsible for everything in your life.'

KEANU

—

He makes statements like: 'When you truly understand karma then you realise you are responsible for everything in your life.' While we latch onto some celebrities because they seem similar to us, perfect to share a couple of wines with in the bar, others are attractive because they're the complete opposite, like Keanu. They've got a special aura.

Teacher, thinker, alien. But somehow Keanu still manages to be down-to-earth: the mystic and adventurer who can still sit on a bench and look sad. He cemented his cinematic status as the perennially restless scholar by learning how to battle demons in *Dracula* and *The Devil's Advocate* and becoming a saviour for the digital age in *Johnny Mnemonic* and *The Matrix.* He became an internet sensation, though, by just being normal.

—

Keanu cuddles puppies. He eats his sandwich on a park bench. He gets melancholy. And whilst 'Sad Keanu' is a little upsetting to see all across Twitter, it's weirdly reassuring too. Seekers like him aren't meant to easily settle. As the man himself said: 'He who loves fifty people has fifty woes; he who loves no one has no woes.'

Or maybe that was the Buddha? Oh well, you know... *they're kind of the same thing.* 'It's nice that people enjoy your work' he has said in typically modest fashion about 'The Cult of Keanu'. Did he really give twenty thousand dollars to a hard-up set builder? Does he genuinely use the subway? Is he actually a mythical being who never ages? We might never get a straight answer but that's what makes Keanu great in the first place. He's not bothered by people thinking he's great.

Which only makes him more great.

When Keanu's suited and booted assassin John Wick growled 'I'm thinking I'm back!' in 2014, it didn't just work for the character, pulled out of retirement to avenge the murder of his pet beagle (obviously). After several years of so-so movies, it was also Keanu the fallen idol declaring his resurrection. And that emphasis on 'I'm *thinking* I'm back'... Did ever a verb sum up someone so well? The badass Wick, all lank locks and dejection, is as meditative as he is murderous, the thinking man's mass killer. I mean, not only was *Chapter 3* of the franchise subtitled in Latin (*Parabellum* – meaning 'prepare for war', as all you Plato fans will know), it also featured a scene where wily Wick picks off baddies using actual books in the hallowed New York Public Library.

Keanu's comeback has been as inspirational as the messages in his movies – he's like a living, breathing affrmation ('Yes I Can-ada!' to quote *Toy Story 4*'s mighty Duke Caboom).

And as both he and his characters continue to wonder – and wander – searching for edification, his legendary Zen-like blankness finds a new wave of popularity in a confused world where we're all desperately searching for answers. Perhaps the answer is, there is no answer? To once again quote the great Ted (quoting the great Socrates): '"The only true wisdom consists in knowing that you know nothing." That's us, dude!'

Who needs Kant and Kierkegaard when we've got Keanu?

—

'"The only true wisdom consists in knowing that you know nothing." That's us, dude!'

TED LOGAN, *BILL & TED'S EXCELLENT ADVENTURE*

—

So here, then, are the teachings of Johns Constantine and Wick, Johnnys Utah and Mnemonic; the musings of Kind Keanu, Kooky Keanu and Kick-Ass Keanu. His movies, moods and mantras have inspired – and crossed – generations and now it's time to celebrate. Following things picked up from Keanu movies – quips, quotes and attitudes – will hopefully help you to move forward along your own happiness path. In Neuro-Linguistic Programming it's known as 'modelling' – essentially imagining yourself in his size tens and asking 'What would Keanu do?'

Now's the chance to find out. Prepare for 'whoa!'

KEANU

THE

GURU

So what is a 'guru'?

What images pop into your head when you hear the word?

A quick picture search on the internet comes up with results that all look remarkably similar. Gurus seem to be lank-haired, bearded men, wandering the Earth with few possessions, inspiring crowds and bringing happiness by calmly saying spiritual things.

Remind you of anyone?

In Sanskrit, the ancient Indian language where the word is believed to have originated, a guru is not just defined as a 'great master' and 'leader' but also a 'dispeller of darkness'; someone who enlightens the ignorant. A guru is ripe with knowledge, like a full cloud.

It's time to face the music: Keanu is a guru. He has the words. He has the knowledge. He has the hair. *Awesome!*

———

Still, even gurus need to start somewhere.

In the first *Matrix* film it's actually Laurence Fishburne as Morpheus who's the *real* guru, not Keanu's Neo. Morpheus is like a walking, talking self-help book; a badass mix of Taekwondo and Tony Robbins (in dodgy shades).

For most of the movie, Neo is us – listening, learning and understandably baffled by the whole concept of 'residual self image' and 'neural interactive simulations'. He asks plenty of questions but doesn't have answers yet. He's not much more than a Ted Logan for the new millennium: a hacker rather than a slacker, maybe... but knowing just as little. 'I'm nobody. I didn't do anything' he pleads. And it's Morpheus who gives him the confidence to face up to the fact that he might, in fact, be the very opposite of 'nobody', that he might be able to learn *and* do. He might have a future as a guru. As 'The One'.

We could all do with a Morpheus in our life. He's the mentor every aspiring guru needs to get them up and running. Or maybe you could be someone else's? So don't just #bemorekeanu. Try being a little Morpheus too. Help turn someone's thought into belief, belief into action.

Older mentors are actually plentiful in Keanu's earlier films – Angelo in *Point Break*, Harry in *Speed*, Rufus in the *Bill & Teds* – although usually he winds up outshining them, obviously. Against expectations too. In 1996's *Chain Reaction* he's Eddie, the lank-haired, plaid shirt-wearing student who looks more like he should be Nirvana's support act than the expert in hydro power that he is. Eventually, though – after several mistakes – he succeeds where mentor Dr Shannon (Morgan Freeman) fails, discovering a way to produce clean energy. The student has become the master.

———

'Try to be wrong once in a while, it'll do your ego good' Keanu once said and it adds up. Making mistakes is an important part of the long journey to guru-dom. Essential, even. Without mistakes there is no learning. Cocking-up every now and then is crucial to growth.

Point Break's Johnny Utah makes umpteen mistakes whilst learning about the surfing robbers known as Ex Presidents ('You know nothing! In fact, you know less than nothing!' he's told). After all, Utah's kind of a square rookie. The Ex Presidents' world of extremes – 100 percent adrenaline – is so alien to him.

Why? Because these revolutionaries think outside of their boxes. Only when the land-locked Utah finally follows suit does he find wisdom in the water, briefly foregoing his conventional life for something more enlightening. Out on the Pacific Ocean, he puts the 'swam' into 'swami'.

Yet it's the early floundering that encourages that focus and determination. Utah has to get to know these guys, get into their heads, embracing their *modus operandi* and experiencing a few stumbles along the way. 'We stand for something' Patrick Swayze's guru-like Bodhi teaches Utah. 'We are here to show those guys that are inching their way on the freeways in their metal coffins that the human spirit is still alive'.

And you can't get more human and spiritual than learning from your mistakes.

———

So what is it that Utah eventually discovers when he's surfing (and, for that matter, Neo when he's karate-kicking, Keanu when he's on his motorbike)?

The answer is perhaps the ultimate guru trait: *flow*.

Flow is being so involved in an activity that nothing else seems to matter, even making it look simple because you've practised so hard after all those early mistakes. It doesn't matter if that activity is physical or mental – it's all about being in the now, connected to this moment. After all, the life we experience is only ever this moment. We really need to bond with it. If you always live for *another* moment then you never really live at all.

Watch Keanu seamlessly kick ass as John Wick and it's a guru in his flow. For a less violent alternative, marvel at Klaatu's equation skills in *The Day the Earth Stood Still*. Flow is the ultimate example of turning your learning into action, mistakes into freedom, and moving forward. Even Keanu's name translates from the Hawaiian as 'cool breeze'. Jeez, the guy's virtually *called* Flow.

In flow you're lost in the moment. It's really the only place worth getting lost in.

WAYS OF FINDING YOUR GURU FLOW, KEANU-STYLE:

1. *Choose goals well.* Goals that are too easy will lead to apathy. Goals that are too difficult are frustrating. So find something in-between, challenging but not overwhelming. 'The path to enlightenment is in the middle way. It is the line between all opposite extremes' as Keanu's Siddhartha says in *Little Buddha*. It could even be just trying to be more mindful in daily life – achievable but certainly not easy.

2. *Meditation.* Take a break to rest the mind, observe thoughts and focus on one thing. It generates calming alpha and theta brain waves and helps you find that all important flow in daily life – a gym session for the brain. There is no 'right' or 'wrong'. It's just a breather. 'Sometimes we get so caught up in our daily lives' Keanu reminds us, 'that we forget to take the time out to enjoy the beauty in life'.

3. *Ritual*. The eye-popping fight between Neo and multiple Agent Smiths in *The Matrix Reloaded* took weeks to perfect. Success doesn't come from what you do occasionally. It comes from what you do consistently. Surfers get up early every day to catch a wave. Fighters train. If Keanu doesn't go exploring on his Norton Commando for a day or two he gets a bit tetchy.

4. *Engage*. To find flow, behave like a traveller not a tourist; make the effort to do, not just look. 'There's a difference between knowing the path and walking the path' Morpheus tells us in *The Matrix*. Maybe it's time to take a stroll?

The message in *Point Break* is clear: for Utah to learn he has to ditch his comfort zone. It makes sense. Meeting new people and learning new skills (be it surfing, kung fu or world history via a time-travelling telephone box) is good for the brain, increasing crucial neural pathways.

—

'Sometimes we get so caught up in our daily lives that we forget to take the time out to enjoy the beauty in life.'

KEANU

—

If you make some mistakes – like falling off your board or having a bromance with a bank robber – don't worry. Keanu himself made some terrible film choices on his way to guru status (*Feeling Minnesota*, anyone?). It's all part of the journey.

'Mohala i ka wai ka maka o ka pua' as Keanu's Hawaiian ancestors might have said. Translation: 'Unfolded by the water are the faces of flowers'. Or, more bluntly, if you want the beauty of a barrel ride, you'll have to get a bit wet.

———

'Try to be wrong once in a while, it'll do your ego good.'
KEANU

Still, being a guru isn't *just* about gaining knowledge from learning and action. It's about the opposite of gaining too.

Yep, gurus know how to *let go*.

Look at Keanu's most inspirational roles and there's one thing they all have in common: these guys rarely have much *stuff*. Outside Bill and Ted's teenage clutter, his characters are ones of thoughts and actions, not possessions.

Take the stunning house owned by John Wick, seriously beautiful in its simplicity, secluded and next to a calming lake. (Where else would a guru live but next to water, one of the most common religious metaphors around, representing such concepts as knowledge, salvation and time?) The main inanimate object that John really cherishes is his Ford Mustang Mach 1, but even that is a carefully chosen vintage piece; strong and durable, not throwaway.

Both John *and* Keanu are the opposite of today's 'fast fashion'. True spiritual teachers like them remove the superfluous, the excess, clearing the path towards the essential. 'Money doesn't mean anything to me' Keanu has claimed. 'I've made a lot of money, but I want to enjoy life and not stress myself building my bank account. I give lots away and live simply, mostly out of a suitcase in hotels. We all know that good health is much more important'.

With such simplicity in his life and films, Keanu becomes the blank onto which we can project our own selves, a clean slate in a black suit (always a black suit!) who's both nothing and everything. He really *is* Utah – one of the biggest states in America and one of the least populated.

Yet in amongst Utah's eighty-five thousand square miles are a rich variety of landscapes: forests, mountains, valleys and deserts. It might seem vast and arid but, really, Utah (from the Apache

Yuttahih, meaning 'one that is higher up')
can do pretty much anything you want it to.

———

'In my quiet, I was working something out.'

KEANU

———

Keanu's simple lifestyle extends into his words too. Or rather, lack of words. 'The secret of being boring' wrote French author Voltaire 'is to say everything', which must make Keanu one of the most interesting people around. He speaks little in films, even less in real life.

Why? Because knowledge is silent. 'In my quiet, I was working something out' Keanu has enigmatically said and it's true that once we realise the power of our thoughts and our words, we cherish them more, favouring silence to the throwaway and the negative. After all, our thoughts and words can create our own weaknesses as well as our own strengths. We need to be careful (it's why 'Excellent!' and 'Whoa!' convey so much more than some lengthy monologue). So work hard in silence. The quieter you become, the more you can hear. Let success be your noise.

And if we can't be quiet, at least we can be straightforward with what we say. An ancient Chinese proverb claims 'Genius can be recognised by its childish simplicity'. Wisdom is concise. And as washed-up quarterback Shane Falco in *The Replacements*, Keanu proves it with his punchy rallying cry: 'Pain heals. Chicks dig scars. Glory... lasts forever'.

Yep, that's pretty basic stuff.

But even the apparently infantile can be insightful when delivered by a guru. Maybe simple Ted has a point in *Bogus Journey* when he claims the lyrics to Poison's power ballad 'Every Rose Has Its Thorn' contain the meaning of life? After all, it's true that to know beauty you must also know pain; to know love, loss.

Or perhaps it's more literal? Next to every wonderful thing there's some prick waiting to hurt you.

———

'The best place to be is here. The best time to be is now.' BILL AND TED, *BILL & TED'S BOGUS JOURNEY*

It's Bill and Ted's treatment of death in *Bogus Journey* that's perhaps the most basic yet guru-like. For those guys, the Grim Reaper is someone to play Twister with, a once intimidating presence to dilute and ultimately befriend. What could be more empowering and enlightening than accepting that the end is inevitable so you might as well have some fun? 'This trip through space and time. It's gonna be over on its own soon enough, isn't it' ponders Keanu's grieving Chris in 1988's teen drama *Permanent Record*. It's a rallying cry to enjoy every moment. 'I came into this thing screaming and kicking. I'm going out the same way'. Or, in the words of Bill and Ted: 'The best place to be is here. The best time to be is now'.

If you can say that about the suburbs of San Dimas then you've truly become a guru.

———

It wasn't until he was in his thirties that the Buddha meditated for forty-nine days under the Bodhi (a tree this time, not Patrick Swayze in *Point Break*), achieving *nirvana* – an extinguishing of lust, hatred and delusion. Meanwhile 5th century BC philosopher Confucius was in his late sixties when he taught disciples about 'the Golden Rule' ('Do not do unto others what you do not want done to yourself'). Aged a whopping ninety-eight years old, V. Nanammal was dubbed 'the Yoga Granny', teaching *asanas* to hundreds of students in Tamil Nadu up until her death in October 2019.

The lesson? Don't hurry or rush. You don't need to keep above fifty miles per hour to find enlightenment.

By 2014 it seemed as if the career of the middle-aged Keanu Reeves had seen better days. Then came *John Wick*: a guru for the greying – determined, focused and still able to scissor sweep the hell out of bad guys young enough to be his kids. Audiences embraced Keanu's maturity, his return to action. He is the Japanese aesthetic concept of *wabi-sabi* in human form: simple, imperfect, marked by the passage of time – and all the more beautiful and spiritual because of it.

'The more sand that has escaped from the hourglass of our life, the clearer we should see through it' wrote the French philosopher and novelist Jean-Paul Sartre. In short: it's never too late to discover yourself and learn (or relearn) these lessons – indeed the later, the better. It's not how old you are, it's how you are old.

So whilst *wabi-sabi* loosely translates as 'rustic serenity', let's make it even more simple by giving it a Keanu spin: *experience is badass*.

———

Okay... you've found your path, you've practised hard, you've meditated regularly and lived a life of modesty and minimalism. What's all that flow actually *for*?

The answer is something that Keanu's seeking out in so many of his films, not to mention every time he heads off into the LA hills on his motorbike: *freedom*. 'When I don't feel free and can't do what I want, I just react' he's admitted. 'I go against it'.

John Wick is a film series all about a man trying to be free (the first shot in *Chapter 3* is of the actual Statue of Liberty). Wick's had enough of the relentless rules in the assassination business and wants to retire, to be his own person again. Winston (Ian McShane) might claim that without rules 'we live with the animals' but that's *exactly* what John wants: to hang out peacefully with his dog.

Freedom is also what the Ex Presidents crave in *Point Break*, what they search for on the waves and in the sky, although Utah's not so sure about the robbing banks part. In 2005's *Constantine*, too, John goes to hell (literally) in a desperate bid to find his ultimate freedom in heaven, discovering along the way that the path to complete independence is a rocky one. 'Getting away from everything feels good' admits Keanu's Scott in early nineties indie classic *My Own Private Idaho*, escaping his stifling family in Portland by riding off on his motorbike, carefree. As Siddhartha in *Little Buddha*, Keanu is even more straight-talking (albeit in a Zen-like way): 'I am looking for freedom'.

And for Bill and Ted, getting sent to the distinctly uptight Oates Military Academy would be, like, *totally bogus*.

Nowhere is that struggle for freedom clearer than in *The Matrix*. 'What is the Matrix?' Morpheus asks, before making things crystal clear: *'Control.'* Here's a film where Neo's own free will is constantly being questioned ('You are a slave, Neo'), the question of who is in charge constantly being posed. Is it man or machine? Taking the enlightening red pill might lead to tough realisations but at least it gives you more freedom than sitting in your office booth all day. Really, has Keanu ever looked more constrained than in those early scenes of *The Matrix*, back when his character is still known as Thomas Anderson, hunched up and working at a desk?

As *The Matrix* series continued, the philosophical wrangling about freedom got more intense, deconstructing old beliefs and asking us to come up with new ones. Influences included more ·isms than you can shake a simulated stick at – Buddhism, Hinduism, Judaism to name just a few – but creators the Wachowskis were deliberate in their scattergun approach to religious nods. They wanted us, the viewers, to grow as Neo did, to go along with him on his journey to guru status, learning from multiple sources. After all, *The Matrix* is a story about minds opening. It needs to welcome all sides.

But most importantly, *The Matrix* is seriously *fun*. Neo's blossoming via kung fu, kissing and 'guns, lots of guns' is a riot to watch. Enlightenment can still be entertaining.

And it's that joy that Keanu's never forgotten. He knows he's a guru to many but he has a laugh with it. 'Do I believe in God, faith, inner faith, the self, passion, and things?' he once laughed. 'Yes, of course! I'm very spiritual... Supremely spiritual... Bountifully spiritual... Supremely bountiful!' After all, what's the point in any spiritual search if you're not going to smile along the way?

Maybe few of us can ever achieve the complete freedom that gurus seek. It's certainly no overnight lightbulb moment. Yet Keanu comes pretty damn close. His deliberate thoughts have led to sincere choices and considered actions. That kind of authenticity is the ultimate form of rebellion.

And whilst we can't all explore big questions in big movies (or on our big motorbikes out in the big Californian countryside) we can at least try in our own small, personal ways. Go for a run. Play chess. Learn to knit. The path to enlightenment looks different to everyone. We just need to take the first step.

#bemorekeanu tips for the wannabe guru:

1. *Learn* **and** *do.* Know the path *and* walk the path. Guru-status is achieved when you stop waiting for the right moment and make the most of the moment you're in now.

2. *Relish mistakes.* Mistakes are helpful in the long-term. Challenges help us understand. Without *The Watcher* (terrible) Keanu might never have made *Something's Gotta Give* (awesome).

3. *Age and experience are a help, not a hindrance.* After all, the higher you've climbed, the better the view.

4. *Find silence.* Every time you return to just the breath, you are experiencing the freedom every guru seeks. The internet has countless useful guided meditations to help.

5. *Simplify, simplify, simplify.* The easiest way to organise your stuff is to get rid of most of it. A simple life is a free life.

'The secret of happiness, you see, is not found in seeking more, but in developing the capacity to enjoy less' claimed Socrates. That's one most non-heinous dude!

KEANU
THE
GENTLEMAN

gentleman *(noun)*

a civilised, educated, sensitive, or well-mannered man

—

Could enlightened, informed and perceptive Keanu be summed up any more accurately?

'Never one to waste words' is how John Wick is described in *Chapter 2* and it's a comment that applies to so many of

Keanu's characters. That famously slow delivery, full of pauses and negative space, might make some think the man's a dunce but really, it's the opposite. Choose what you say carefully and everyone listens. Sentences gain weight that way. For a movie star, it gives presence, atmosphere and dynamism. It makes Keanu a wonderful conundrum. Has there ever been another action man who's so sporty (kung fu, hockey, surfing, football) whilst seeming so sluggish?

Yet by slowing down our behaviour with awareness, we can process our emotions more clearly and more healthily (and John Wick has a *lot* of emotions to process). Those films might be fast and flashy but John's attitude is a tribute to a more considered, slower-paced way of life. I mean, he even killed someone with a *pencil*. How much more old-school can you get?

Okay, maybe killing someone with a book, as happens in *Chapter 3*...

Of course Keanu doesn't *usually* use books to end lives. Reading is like a journey to a new place and, as a well-rounded gent, he's more than happy to use pages to expand his world view. 'Every moment is precious. I'm trying to travel. I want to go to Paris... I'd like to read some books' he told *Interview* magazine in November 1991.

In preparation for *My Own Private Idaho*, Keanu gorged on John Rechy novels, one of the pioneers of LGBT literature. Other favourite authors include Philip K. Dick, John Updike and Fyodor Dostoevsky, writers who challenge and examine. The latter's *The Idiot* is about 'a truly beautiful soul' whose goodness is in stark contrast with a corrupt world. I wonder why Keanu empathises with a story like that?

WHY THE BEST PEOPLE READ (BOOKS, NOT JUST BUZZFEED):

1. *It's mentally stimulating.* Reading is a neurological workout that keeps your brain in shape.

2. *It's relaxing* – a distraction from real world stress.

3. *It's educational.* Books boost knowledge and vocabulary.

4. *It helps concentration.* Read more and improve your ability to focus.

Hey, you're reading *this* book so that's a start.

———

There's still one vital thing missing from the dictionary definition of 'gentleman', though: *Must love dogs*.

It's true: canine companions in Keanu movies are crucial to his classiness. In *The Lake House* a pet pooch is there to show us that whilst Alex is single, he's no oddball. In *Feeling Minnesota*, a doggy companion offsets the fact that Keanu is actually playing an ex-con. In 2001's *Sweet November*, his advertising exec Nelson is a dick when he doesn't like dogs, a dude when he does.

When a violent assassin like John Wick – a man who ends a hundred and twenty-eight lives in just the second film alone – is seen adoring his pet beagle Daisy (a present from his late wife), it's to reveal his gentlemanly side, that he's emotional too. For a movie hardman to have a heart, he definitely needs a hound. The responsibility of caring for a dog is just too good for your mental health to not use it as movie shorthand for 'don't worry everyone – this guy's okay'. Pets equal decency.

A video featuring Keanu surrounded by puppies ('Look how cute you are!') has well over thirteen million views on YouTube. The lesson? Never underestimate the appeal of a gent cuddling Labradors.

———

For Keanu's most considerate and gentlemanly role, look no further than Dr Julian Mercer in *Something's Gotta Give*. Julian is the dreamy, dashing, Freud-quoting lifesaver that falls for Diane Keaton's klutzy Erica, twenty years his senior. 'You really are a very sexy woman' he purrs earnestly.

Of course age doesn't matter to an open-minded healer like Julian. He sees beyond the conventions of age-appropriateness, a fanboy utterly in awe of Erica's maturity. Even – spoiler alert! – when Julian finds himself competing for Erica's affections with ageing playboy Harry (Jack Nicholson), he's still entirely understanding of the whole situation. Not even a cross word. A female fantasy from writer/director Nancy Meyers, maybe, yet – as life coaches like to say – whatever the mind can conceive, it can achieve. Julian doesn't have to be just a fictional joke, he can be a realistic goal too. A barometer of kindness and humility to aim for.

I bet he'd be kind to dogs too.

———

Keanu's strong, silent gentleman roles like Julian are all about goodness and thankfully he brings that goodness to his real life too. In 2019 his kindness even earned him the nickname of 'the internet's boyfriend', revelations of sweet behaviour flooding social media (such as taking pay cuts on films to help out behind-the-scenes crews).

He claims it's his British heritage that instilled him with those famous good manners, although the revelation that he considerately never touches women's lower backs whilst posing in photos with them also has roots in his Asian heritage (it's known as the 'manner hands' in South Korea). So playing an understanding doctor in not just *Something's Gotta Give* but also in anorexia drama *To the Bone* makes complete sense really. Keanu's whole life is based on a kindly bedside manner.

—

'I was also raised to treat people exactly how I would like to be treated by others. It's called respect.'

KEANU

—

'There is no need for temples; no need for complicated philosophy. Our own brain, our own heart is our temple; the philosophy is kindness' said the Dalai Lama. And Keanu's right there with the exiled spiritual leader of Tibetan Buddhism when it comes to simple good behaviour: 'I was also raised to treat people exactly how I would like to be treated by others. It's called respect'. There's a generosity outside of being a movie star, too. He's anonymously donated to multiple charities and has been filmed offering his seat on the Brooklyn-bound Q train to a lady weighed down with bags. (Mind you, watch the action-packed subway scenes in *The Matrix*, *Speed* and *John Wick: Chapter 2* and you might not want Keanu anywhere near you on public transport.) When his flight from San Francisco to Los Angeles had to make an emergency landing over a hundred miles from its destination, Keanu helped sort a bus replacement service, regaling passengers with stories and music for the two hour drive. As a champion of independent bookstores and publishers, Keanu started up his own 'esoteric' imprint, X Artists' Books, with future partner Alexandra Grant. And as his date for the 2020 Academy Awards he brought along Patricia Taylor – his mum.

Unexpected political and medical events in the twenty-first century have affected all of us. Many therapists are even advising we take a break from the doom-laden media to avoid excessive anxiety. It's why the positive stories about Keanu make such an impact; even 'Keanu doing things' memes are small beacons of light in dark times. When turbulence seems overwhelming, it's important to remember what unites us rather than what divides: a kind and quiet man who loves canines. '... an unlikely antidote to everything wrong with the news cycle?' asked the journalist Naomi Fry in the spring of 2019: 'the actor Keanu Reeves.'

———

From the bonds formed as part of an ice hockey team at school to those created whilst playing in a band, Keanu is the loner who's still happy to collaborate. You can see it in the times he's been part of an ensemble cast (*Much Ado About Nothing*, *The Gift*) or played a supporting role (*Toy Story 4*) or cameo (*Always Be My Maybe*) – an unusually modest move for a bona fide leading man.

Collaboration is key to open-minded behaviour. A group environment – everyone working towards the same goal – promotes friendship, loyalty and motivation. It's perfect, too, for hearing other views and meeting people with different experiences. It's all there in Keanu's frequent praise for his stunt team (yes, he gave each of his stunt crew on *The Matrix* sequels a £6,000 Harley Davidson). It's a recognition that success is so often because of a larger effort rather than an individual ego. 'Workplace synergy' they call it in business. Or as Keanu puts it (when talking about working with his stunt team on the *John Wick* movies): 'That feeling, that bond, of just like "Wow, we did that! That was great!"'

In *Bill & Ted's Excellent Adventure* – a film entirely about a random group of people cooperating for a common good – the boys sum it up even more simply: 'Be excellent to each other!'

———

Keanu has been quietly, excellently, working with female directors ever since a 28-year-old Marisa Silver cast him in her film *Permanent Record* in 1988. These days, at a time when only around eight percent of movie directors in Hollywood are women, Keanu's collaboration rate is double that – claimed to be the highest for any A-list male star. 'It's always wonderful to get to know women, with the mystery and the joy and the depth' he stated, melting a million hearts in the process.

'I've known him for over twenty years and he has been consistently the same person in the most beautiful way' says Charlize Theron, a co-star in two movies. 'Of course he's grown and all that stuff that happens in twenty years but his core, his heart, his soul, his kindness, his generosity, his sweetness has just always been so consistent. I love that about him'.

Okay, she has a different opinion of him in *The Devil's Advocate*, the morality tale of a kind country lawyer (Keanu) who signs up with a rich – but nefarious – big city firm with a devilish boss (Al Pacino), much to the frustration of his wife Mary Ann (Charlize). 'It's blood money, Kevin. And we just drank it down, both of us' she complains. Riffing on biblical theology, Dante's 'Inferno' and *Paradise Lost*, *The Devil's Advocate* is a nineties thriller with a shockingly contemporary hook: what happens when Satan himself is in a position of earthly power? (and yes, the future POTUS 45 even gets a mention).

Pacino lays out the central issue on a plate, foreshadowing today's era of 'selfie culture': 'Vanity... is definitely my favourite sin. Kevin, it's so basic, self-love; the all-natural opiate. You know, it's not that you didn't care for Mary Ann, Kevin. It's just that you were a little bit more involved with someone else: yourself.'

In other words, Kevin forgot his manners.

But of course the movie's about him learning a lesson from all this chaos, changing his mind and rediscovering his good behaviour. Even a gentleman – *especially* a gentleman – has to keep learning.

Temptations are normal, of course. No one's perfect – not even Keanu. But there are ways to avoid them. Experts recommend that the first thing to do when aiming to resist temptation is to set achievable goals. Don't say 'I won't spend any more time looking at pictures of Keanu online *ever*' – just say 'I won't spend *the next hour* looking at pictures of Keanu online'. Be realistic. By admitting it's down to the choices you make, you're taking control of the situation. 'I'm an architect' Keanu tells us as Evan in 2015's *Knock Knock*, 'so obviously I believe in things happening by your own design.' Choose that design wisely.

———

—

'If you have been brutally broken but still have the courage to be gentle to other living beings, then you're a badass with a heart of an angel.'

KEANU

—

'Grief changes shape. But it never ends' Keanu believes. And it's true that if you love, you will grieve. It's one of life's certainties.

Death seems to be constantly hanging over Keanu's characters – John Wick and Constantine, Nelson in *Sweet November*, William in 2018's *Replicas*, even Ted in *Bogus Journey* – yet the way that he faces loss in his films and, tragically, in his real life shows a high degree of emotional sophistication. 'He who mourns, mends' goes the old saying and Keanu is someone unafraid to take measures to ensure grief is eventually reconciled into his life, rather than burying feelings.

In *John Wick* he chooses quiet and solitude to help him through that mourning, reclusively protective of his time and the house that brought him and wife Helen comfort. In his own life, after the death of close friend River Phoenix in 1993, aged just 23, Keanu chose work to honour his friend – one of the most naturally talented actors of his generation.

Keanu's mid-nineties were proof that strength truly emerges when we're being tested, that grief can bring down the walls we all put up and reveal us at our most raw. The trio of films that quickly followed Phoenix's passing – *Speed*, *Johnny Mnemonic* and *A Walk in the Clouds* – weren't all great but are among Keanu's most varied; the product of someone channelling their despair into creativity; a fighter more tough than any clichéd movie action man, a gentleman using his choices carefully. 'If you have been brutally broken but still have the courage to be gentle to other living beings' he's claimed, 'then you're a badass with a heart of an angel'.

Unfortunately, worse was still to come. During Christmas 1999, Keanu's daughter with girlfriend Jennifer Syme was stillborn. The romance soon broke down under the strain and Jennifer herself lost her life in a car accident in 2001. Around the same time Keanu's sister Kim was diagnosed with leukaemia. His coping mechanism?

He took time away from relationships to fully heal and used his money to provide financial support for Kim and others like her.

'I miss all the great things that will never be' Keanu said of his losses – and certainly our scars don't disappear entirely. Yet we *can* change how we see them.

Tending to others is one way, since it helps to reframe our own problems. Getting creative is another. For Keanu 'making art is about trying to find the good in people and making the world a more compassionate place' and as an actor, he's even used the lessons he's learned from personal tragedy to help understand certain film parts: 'With any character, the way I think about it is, you have the role on the page, you have the vision of the director and you have your life experience'.

So be kind to others, yes, but be kind to yourself too. Embracing heartbreak graciously like that isn't just a way to survive it – it's a way for you to develop. Not every storm comes to drown us. Some come to clear the way ahead. Loss changes us but over time we can learn from it, emerging with a new outlook. It's right there in the plot of *The Day the Earth Stood Still*: we tend to struggle to evolve unless we're challenged (such as when an angry alien who looks exactly like Keanu lands in New York).

And afterwards, time will always heal any wounds. 'Everything flows and nothing abides, everything gives way and nothing stays fixed' proclaimed ancient Greek philosopher Heraclitus the Obscure. Keanu the Gentleman said it more clearly: 'Even in the face of tragedy, a stellar person can thrive. No matter what's going on in your life, you can overcome it! Life is worth living'.

And it's even better with a dog.

—

'Even in the face of tragedy, a stellar person can thrive. No matter what's going on in your life, you can overcome it! Life is worth living.'

KEANU

—

#bemorekeanu tips for wannabe gentlefolk:

1. *Speak a little, say a lot.* Listen more, consider your thoughts, be concise. It's not just the polite thing to do. It shows emotional maturity and seriousness too.

2. *Reading is growing.* It's travel for the brain, broadening horizons, where learning and humility meet.

3. *Be generous.* To others and to yourself. Focusing on other people's problems will reframe your own. Being patient with yourself allows time to heal.

4. *Accept evolution.* From suffering we learn compassion – and more – so why fight it? Kindness adapts.

5. *Rescue a dog (optional).* But always remember: puppies are for life, not just for YouTube.

There's an old proverb that says 'Better good manners than good looks' but the two don't have to be mutually exclusive. Good manners *are* good looking. Gentility charms. It wasn't just Keanu's *Speed* biceps that got him nominated at the 1996 MTV Movie Awards as 'Most Desirable Male'.

KEANU

THE

FIGHTER

Keanu doesn't play backstreet brawlers. His fighters live with honour, follow codes. The buzz word in *John Wick: Chapter 3* is 'fealty', a phrase that originated in the Middle Ages, meaning loyalty to a leader. Even kung fu – a technique that is rumoured to have started over four thousand years ago – translates from Chinese as 'achievement' or 'hard work'.

In short: you can't become a badass without breaking a sweat, without learning the rules.

The gag in *The Matrix* might be that Neo acquires umpteen *wushu* skills from a quick upload to his brain ('I know kung fu!') but in reality Keanu was put through the grind for months to get it right. And whilst we might not all have renowned martial arts choreographers to help us with our flying kicks, the principle remains the same: a fight master is a practitioner... who keeps practising.

Or, as John Wick is so poetically described: 'A man of focus, commitment and sheer ****ing will'.

The guy's certainly put in the hours. As a retired assassin dragged back into the job to get revenge, Wick's mission is to show the young pretenders what drive and determination really look like; a Rocky-like relic, forced to defend the honour (and beagle) of his late wife. He's reluctant, yes. But that never makes him sloppy.

Or rude. In *Chapter 2*, John even pours a drink for the dodgy Tarasov, carefully and kindly pushing the glass across a desk to him before going off to wipe out most of the gangster's men. Service before self. It's just basic manners. 'Sometimes enemies are our best teachers' believes Keanu, offering respect to even those that have hurt him. 'People can learn from their mistakes, destruction sometimes means rebirth'. Every fight is an opportunity.

Plus, of course, those fights aren't just physical. The strongest people are those in the middle of battles we don't even see. The fight to get on with life – get up, go to work, cook the meal – when mental darkness has set in is as big a struggle as anything John Wick faces. The brain is the first muscle we need to build to achieve anything, whether it's beating up the bad guys or simply greeting each day with a smile.

———

One of the easier ways to #bemorekeanu is to follow the fighter's exercise regime he used for *John Wick*.

KEANU'S 'YOU STOLE MY CAR AND YOU KILLED MY DOG' WICK-OUT ROUTINE:

- choose low-impact circuit training rather than just one or two intense exercises.

- perform twenty reps of each move.

- only rest very briefly between them.

- when the first circuit is done, take a two minute breather.

- repeat five more times (with two minute breaks).

- beat up a bunch of gangsters in your front room.

Okay, so the last one isn't essential but the benefits of exercise like that are useful whether you're a pissed-off assassin or not: weight control, lower risk of heart disease, enhanced alertness, strengthened bones and muscles, raised libido and improved mental health.

Especially mental health. Keanu's commitment to his action roles is never only about the body. Training for *John Wick* wasn't about pumping iron. It was about movement, muscular endurance and stability. The goal was to get Keanu into a mindset as much as one of those slim-fit suits. 'That's not just physical. That's mental. That's a certain kind of mental fortitude' *John Wick* co-director Chad Stahelski told *GQ*, when discussing his star's fitness plan.

It worked. When footage of the actor seamlessly flowing through weapons practice turned up online, the response was predictably huge. Here was the perfect example of the physical and the mental working together, Keanu displaying both the body *and* brain skills it takes to inhabit a character such as Wick. It's his search for authenticity at its most dedicated.

Yet *John Wick*'s helmers David Leitch and Chad Stahelski still wanted to train their star even harder than on previous films, giving him *new* challenges to make this outing extra spectacular. So whilst the visuals in *John Wick* may be hi-tech, behind the scenes there's an old message about dedication to self-improvement. Live a life of learning and curiosity – train your brain – and your body will be prepared for anything.

'Water shapes its course according to the nature of the ground over which it flows' wrote ancient Chinese strategist Sun Tzu. 'The soldier works out his victory in relation to the foe whom he is facing'. In other words, adapt or die. Research even suggests that the sense of purpose associated with constantly trying new things like this – adapting and evolving – leads to lower cortisol levels, better immune function and more efficient sleep.

In that case, Keanu must sleep like a baby.

—

'Water shapes its course according to the nature of the ground over which it flows. The soldier works out his victory in relation to the foe whom he is facing.'

SUN TZU

—

As much as training and rules matter, the best fighter won't ignore their instinct. *Speed*'s Jack Traven is a 'hotshot', full of academy-learned seriousness, in no mood for the frivolous game-playing of Dennis Hopper's Howard Payne (in the backside). Yet Jack's strength is as much from what he *feels* as what he knows. Education is one thing – so is practising a new skill – but here's instinct at its most powerful. 'Do not attempt to grow a brain' he's told sarcastically and it's kind of true: Jack is Keanu at his most elemental, taking risks as much as challenging his intellect. 'You're not too bright, man' Howard goes on. 'But you got some big, round, hairy cojones'.

So for all the rules and repetition – crucial as foundations to learning – sometimes you just have to rely on quick thinking and listening to your gut, too.

And yes – having some big (metaphorical) bollocks.

Some of those instincts are hardwired in your body, of course. There's no thinking involved. Hear a sudden loud noise, for example, and you'll react with a jump – it's automatic. Nevertheless, instincts can still be honed; they're still linked to our learning and experience and all that mental strength the best fighters cultivate. So relying on instinct doesn't mean you don't need to do your homework. It's not a shortcut. Jack Traven trained, trained and trained so that he could be sure of what his senses were telling him on board that number 2525 bus.

And science is on our side. Research shows human intuition like that has our long term goals in its interest. So listen to your gut and its 100 million nerve cells. It's no wonder it's often referred to as 'the second brain' with that kind of communicative power. It instinctively knows what's best for our survival. *Excellent!*

———

What's a bigger myth than any tale the Wachowskis could come up with?

Multi-tasking.

It's simply not efficient and the well-trained, instinctive warrior knows it. They have a single objective, a concrete goal that they get on with achieving. They don't let themselves get bogged down with details and distractions. Fighters see the big picture, the end goal. They don't try to multi-task.

Why? Research in neuroscience finally has the answer, stating that the brain doesn't *actually* perform multiple tasks simultaneously – we just switch between them quickly. It's a stop/start process. And the surprise to many? Flip-flopping like that is less effective than focusing on one thing at a time since we make more mistakes, it drains more energy and actually costs vital seconds. Keanu may be able to beat up more than one baddie at a time but he remains single-minded: stop the robbers, avenge a death, keep that bus going...

If focusing on a big goal like that feels intimidating, try taking the warrior route and breaking it down into 'micro' goals; several mini-goals that are individually easier to digest. When Neo fights hundreds of Agent Smiths in *The Matrix Reloaded* he's not actually fighting 'hundreds of Agent Smiths'. He's fighting one Agent Smith hundreds of times.

All of which makes it kind of ironic that Keanu has become an internet phenomenon – a gift to gif-givers and meme-makers – since in real life he's way too focused on important things than on something flippant like social media. He's too busy tackling those micro goals to bother with Likes, Views and Retweets. If Keanu doesn't have FOMO (Fear of Missing Out) then he doesn't have JOMO (Joy of Missing Out) either – because he doesn't even think he's missing out on anything.

For Keanu, it's all about JOHN (Joy of Having Nothing).

That's a wise move. Avoiding the constant distraction of the internet can be good for everyone. Quitting that addiction to quick hits of information increases patience and focus. Saying goodbye to the myth of multi-tasking makes every fight a whole lot more simple. 'I will search for you through a thousand worlds and ten thousand lifetimes until I find you' said Keanu's samurai Kai in *47 Ronin*. Let's be honest: that kind of commitment has no space for selfies.

'I will search for you through a thousand worlds and ten thousand lifetimes until I find you.'

KAI, *47 RONIN*

You can measure how brave you are by how vulnerable you're willing to be. And whilst Keanu's action scenes have become fan favourites, it's his emotional openness – on film and in real life – that show his real strength. True heroes are willing to lay bare their emotions and say things such as 'I don't want to be part of a world where kindness is a weakness' (yep, that's Keanu).

No-one can be truly strong unless they allow themselves to be vulnerable too. After all, you can never improve wellness if you refuse to talk about yourself. Yes, judgement from others might be a worry when we open up but really, where's the shame in admitting your flaws? It actually shows a strong emotional maturity. Refusing to be vulnerable means locking up your truths – but they can't stay locked up forever. Repression like that only leads to pain (even more pain than an ass-whooping from Agent Smith).

So be kind to yourself by being honest.

It'll probably be a fight at first, but only openness can lead to real strength. Allowing love and kindness into your life like that also allows others in. And what's stronger than a single person? A community. A union.

'Being deeply loved by someone gives you strength, while loving someone deeply gives you courage' wrote the Chinese philosopher Lao Tzu. And it's finally being open to love that gives Neo his drive in *The Matrix* – his strength, his courage, his powerful humanity. 'It's pointless to keep fighting' snarls Agent Smith. 'Why, Mr Anderson? Why? Why do you persist?'

Neo's reply is full of strength, bravery and joyful free will: 'Because I choose to.'

———

'Sometimes enemies are our best teachers.' KEANU

#bemorekeanu tips for wannabe warriors:

1. *Focus and commit.* A fighter never stops training. 'I fear not the man who has practised 10,000 kicks once' said Bruce Lee. 'I fear the man who has practised one kick 10,000 times.'

2. *Adapt.* Whether your battle is physical or mental, things change. Goalposts move. Parameters shift. Be prepared to move with them.

3. *Trust your gut.* Instinct is inherent but can also be sharpened. The more you practise something, the more your intuition is likely to be right.

4. *Treat the brain as a muscle.* A true warrior knows that their brain needs to be exercised too, that struggles are won when head, heart and hand all work together.

5. *Log off.* I mean, did you ever see John Wick check his Instagram?

'Victory belongs to the most persevering' said the great military general Napoleon. He should know. He persevered at Austerlitz in 1805, Friedland in 1807 and Waterloo – one of San Dimas's most excellent water parks – in 1988.

KEANU
THE
FRIEND

Sorry Woody and Buzz but Bill and Ted have the best movie bromance of all time.

If their *Excellent Adventure* is about anything, it's about friendship – one that can survive the maelstrom of time-travelling chaos being thrown at them. The boys' era-hopping transforms a suburban San Dimas shopping mall into a swirling melting pot of nods and name-drops that really shouldn't be hanging out together (Joan of Arc and aerobics?). Yet the wonder and smiles of our teenage heroes rarely falter; eighties optimists in a decade whose rampant pop culture was confusing for many (not least Keanu in his brilliantly bleak breakthrough film, *River's Edge*).

For Bill and Ted, though, all that mess is a simple invitation to 'Party on!' And whatever life throws at you – band practice, history homework, a hot stepmother – never stop being excellent to each other.

Messrs Logan & Preston: therapists to the nation's youth.

———

excellent *(adjective)*

possessing outstanding quality; superior merit; remarkably good

———

Teenage life isn't often 'remarkably good'. Keanu himself had spent his early years unsettled after his parents' break-up. At the movies, early gigs included some tough roles in some tough films. His late eighties cohorts meanwhile – Johnny, Ethan, River – seemed chock full of adolescent angst.

Bill and Ted, though... they wouldn't even be able to *pronounce* angst. Their minds are on other things ('69, dudes!').

When French philosophers wrote about the 1980s they used words like 'fragmentary', 'disposable' and 'promiscuous' – hardly a ringing endorsement of an era. But what Bill and Ted celebrate, as twentieth-century boys leaping through an eye-popping range of timelines, is the very opposite of anything so fleeting and negative. They might have been flunking their traditional history class but their unfettered enthusiasm, fuelled by friendship, meant the pressures of teenage life soon melted away.

And *that's* what being excellent actually means: politeness, joy and friendship. *Excellent Adventure* is an early indicator of Kind Keanu – a film where virtue, comradeship and community win out over material wealth (although a couple of new 'Flying V' guitars are always nice). Really, it's a childlike innocence, one as old as their pal Socrates and his own Ancient Greek thoughts about best buds: 'There is no possession more valuable than a good and faithful friend'.

That dude knew what he was talking about.

Find someone you'd be willing to give your Megadeth collection to. Close friendships have been shown in many studies to have a profound effect on both mental and physical wellbeing, even helping you live longer. *Whoa!*

——

'[*Excellent Adventure*] had a sweetness, an idiosyncrasy, it didn't have a lick of cynicism in it and I think that was really refreshing... it's a movie about friendship and I think that connected with people.'

ALEX WINTER

Friendship is everywhere in *Excellent Adventure*, not budging even as Beethoven, Freud and Joan of Arc – who *wasn't* Noah's wife – hang out in the present day and virtually take over San Dimas. Socrates and Billy the Kid palling up to flirt with girls in the local mall is a particular highlight – a triumph of optimism. Who says an ancient Greek philosopher and a Wild West outlaw can't be mates?

And it wasn't just the title characters themselves who were BFFs but Keanu and his co-star Alex Winter too; both the same age, both into motorbikes, both growing up outside of America before moving there as children (Winter was born in England). They would still play air guitar riffs together when the film wasn't shooting. Even writers Chris Matheson and Ed Solomon were college besties.

Meanwhile George Carlin, as Rufus, was nearly thirty years older than the boys but they still bonded. 'He's this larger than life, beautiful, spiritual, incredible human being' Keanu told *Entertainment Weekly*. Perhaps their friendship shouldn't be a complete surprise. As a legendary counterculture comedian, Carlin made you laugh and think at the same time. 'We've added years to life, not life to our years' he claimed. 'Trying to be happy by accumulating possessions is like trying to satisfy hunger by taping sandwiches all over your body.' He was being more Keanu before Keanu was even born.

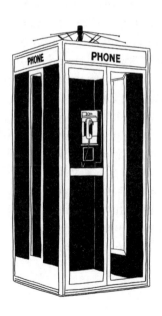

'[*Excellent Adventure*] had a sweetness, an idiosyncrasy, it didn't have a lick of cynicism in it and I think that was really refreshing... it's a movie about friendship and I think that connected with people' Alex Winter believes. It's no wonder he and Keanu returned nearly thirty years later for *Bill & Ted Face the Music*. Working with your mates makes sense. It's proven to generate more job satisfaction thanks to feelings of increased trust and loyalty, which in itself leads to greater productivity. It's all in the chemistry. The oxytocin and serotonin produced when talking with friends are important mood optimisers.

So whilst being more Keanu might mean times of silence and solitude, when it comes to the power of old friendships, even Mr Reeves himself recognises the benefits. Chad Stahelski, before directing the *John Wick* series, was Keanu's stunt co-ordinator on *Point Break* and *The Matrix* films whilst Keanu and pal Winona Ryder have been in three movies together.

The rumours are, thanks to a wedding scene in *Bram Stoker's Dracula* that was conducted by a real priest, they might even be *actually* married. And hey, it wouldn't be so bad, if true. After all, Winona has admitted: 'I just love being together with him so much'.

—

It's hard not to think about all the films Keanu and his late buddy River Phoenix might have made.

It was River's girlfriend Martha Plimpton and his brother Leaf (aka Joaquin) who were friends with Keanu first, thanks to their working together on the movie *Parenthood* in 1989. 'Then I met up with him on *I Love You to Death*' River explained to *Interview* magazine a few years later. 'And I liked the guy. I wanted to work with him. He's like my older brother'.

Keanu was so inspired by the script of *My Own Private Idaho* that he rode over a thousand miles on his motorbike to give it to River. Later River helped Keanu get into the right zone for the tender arthouse film at a time when he'd only just finished filming its polar opposite: the high-octane *Point Break*. It was a partnership; you can see it in the film, read it in the interviews they did together at the time. A love.

Realising the power of true friendship – and the sadness when someone decides to end it – is what *My Own Private Idaho* is ultimately all about. Neither Keanu nor River came from conventional families and their characters Scott and Mike are the same; drifters, searching for answers.

So if you can't rely on your family, form your own surrogate one from friends. After all, friends don't have all the Freudian complexities that families have ('My dad doesn't know that I'm just a kid' Scott says in the film. 'He thinks I'm a threat'). Or as Keanu's character Tod proclaims in *Parenthood*: '... you need a licence to buy a dog, or drive a car. Hell, you need a licence to catch a fish! But they'll let any butt-reaming asshole be a father!'

Not all of us are born into the families that are the best for us. Yet we all have the ability to cultivate the friendships that are exactly that. Look at the relationship between Tod and Garry (Keanu and Leaf) in *Parenthood* – a simple and strong surrogate father/son bond in a comedy all about the complexities of blood ties.

Plus, of course, your best friend doesn't even have to be human. Just ask John Wick.

———

A good friend – male, female or canine – broadens your world view.

As *Point Break*'s undercover cop Johnny Utah begins to bond with his target – bad-boy surfer Bodhi – the lawman starts to question his own existence. Like Bodhi, he's also a rebel in his field. Maybe the two of them could be genuine friends? Let's be honest, riding waves and jumping out of planes together looks one helluva lot of fun.

Utah's admiration for Bodhi blossoms into something as close to homoerotic desire as director Kathryn Bigelow could get away with in a mainstream action movie. 'I know it's hard for you, Johnny! I know you want me so bad it's like acid in your mouth'

Bodhi taunts his police pal. The fact that Utah struggles to go all the way with arresting his man – suggestively firing bullets into the sky rather than at his target – doesn't matter. The genuine friendship between the two of them – that almost-romance that's at the heart of a fanciful plot about bank robbers and kidnapping – has opened Utah's mind. He's discovered something new about himself. Whether that's the joy of surfing or that he actually fancies dudes is up to us to decide.

Today's social media can never replace that authenticity and intimacy of face-to-face interactions – of looking someone in the eyes as you're free-falling from an aeroplane together. The best friends aren't virtual ones. A real presence can motivate us, improve our wellbeing… and help us realise deeply buried things about ourselves.

———

Making friends as a grown-up can admittedly be an odd experience. For starters we just don't meet as many new people as adults. Plus, our awareness is likely to have changed. Children make friends with fewer inhibitions, largely because their relationships are focused on play. As adults, unless we're surfing bank-robbers, we're less likely to be so carefree. After all, we worry about looking foolish if we ask someone out on a romantic date and they say no – and it's no different in the search for a new platonic relationship.

Not every friendship has to be like Utah and Bodhi of course, yet experts claim that to find new friends as an adult, a certain amount of *Point Break*-style wooing is required.

'There is no possession more valuable than a good and faithful friend.'

SOCRATES

SOME TIPS FOR DEALING WITH A PNF (POTENTIAL NEW FRIEND):

- *Once you've identified a PNF, don't be afraid to flirt a little.* Flirting is dipping a toe in the water, getting on a surfboard for the first time and seeing how it feels. Look for shared interests, values and emotions by casually throwing them into conversation.

- *If that goes well, consider the next step.* How will you spend more time with your PNF? Treat it as you would a romantic date. Try new experiences together or introduce your PNF to a pastime that has personal meaning to you. Over time you'll get to know if they are 'the one' (sorry Neo).

- *Are they as interested in your life as you are theirs?* Friendships – like romance – need balance.

- *Friendships also need work.* Check-in on friends (new and old) out of the blue, support their plans, push them when you think they need it. The best ones, like Keanu and Charlize, can even withstand a little time apart.

'I can literally see him and we pick up right from where we left off' Theron has admitted. 'He's one of those friends that, it's fine if we don't see each other for a year. Then we'll hang out and I can't even remember that time passing between us. I love him'. Did you know that Charlize even has a dog called Johnny Utah?

If you work from your authenticity like that, you tend to attract the right people. Keanu isn't known for having lots of friends but that only makes the ones that he *does* have all the more true. Most importantly he's always remembered one simple fact: whether your friendship is brand new, began on the set of *The Devil's Advocate* or even dates back to your teen years at San Dimas High, never, ever stop being excellent to each other.

#bemorekeanu tips for being the Bill to someone's Ted (or the other way around):

1. *Party on!* Optimism in the face of overwhelming odds (such as Evil Bill and Evil Ted trying to stop you winning the Battle of the Bands contest) is the mark of a most bodacious compadre.

2. *Work on projects together.* Because what's good for the head and heart is also good for business.

3. *Learn and teach.* Close friends can open our minds to new ideas – and we can do the same for them. 'A wise man is he who listens to counsel' it says in the Bible (from the days when women obviously weren't allowed to be seen as wise).

4. *Flirt.* Finding new friends takes a bit of emotional work, as does keeping the old ones. If it feels right, the effort won't feel like a chore.

5. *'Be excellent to each other!'* Obviously.

'Chris and I have remarked that if all we ever did was put the phrase "Be Excellent To Each Other" into the world, it wouldn't be so bad' admits *Bill & Ted* co-writer Ed Solomon. And he's got a point. When you can choose anything in this world, why not choose kindness?

KEANU

THE

ROCKSTAR

As the great 'Dave Beeth Oven' once said: 'Music is... a higher revelation than all wisdom and philosophy'. And that dude knew how to rock.

Numerous tests have shown that music can lift our moods, help combat depression, improve blood flow, lower levels of stress-related hormones, even ease pain. It's why scientists have studied the effect of music on patients before, during and after surgery.

The result? A reduction in anxiety and discomfort. Music's more than just pressing 'Play' on the latest Spotify playlist. It's therapy.

A QUICK GUIDE TO LISTENING TO MUSIC THERAPEUTICALLY. (IT'S GREAT FOR FINDING YOUR FLOW.):

1. *Listen out for repetition.* Which melodies come back? How do they shift and change?

2. *How does the song use space and silence?* How does doing less make more impact?

3. *How dense does the song sound?* Is it a warm 'Wall of Sound' production or, like Keanu's favourites Joy Division, sparse and sinister?

4. *Which moments are planned, which improvised?* Listen out for elements you think are off-the-cuff and the most authentic.

Using music to express your individuality – through listening to it or, even more, through playing it – is also a way to advertise your strengths to others. In evolutionary terms, it's to show that you'd be a good mating partner. Yes, if you've wondered why Keanu looks extra attractive when he's strapped to a bass guitar, the answer's surprisingly simple: it's his mating call.

Making music shows off creativity and prowess in the most blatant context: on a stage, with people staring at you, weighing you up. It's a way of letting possible partners know you exist and that you're a good team player. Play music to someone and their brain releases chemicals that make them feel pleasure, excitement and satisfaction.

Keanu has long known of music's magic, of course. One of his earliest lead roles was in *Permanent Record*, the story of a high-school rock band coming to terms, through music, with the suicide of their lead songwriter. In his first scene he's in his boxers, playing guitar. Shortly after he's breaking into a studio to meet Lou Reed. Hard to believe, maybe, but it's a relentless passion for music that helps him with the loss of his best friend. It's music as a spiritual guide; kind of *Bill & Ted's Existential Adventure*.

'Music gives soul to the universe' wrote the great philosopher Plato. It's 'the strongest form of magic' said another (well, Marilyn Manson). Whether your tastes are Ancient Greek or Industrial Metal, one thing's for sure: God gave rock 'n' roll to us.

———

'Music gives soul to the universe.'

PLATO

Bill and Ted aren't very good at playing guitar but it doesn't matter. It's their love of music, not their skill, that unites them. Being from the future, Rufus knows that one day Bill and Ted's musical partnership 'will align the planets and bring them into universal harmony' (spoiler alert: that gets hastily sorted at the end of *Bogus Journey*) but until then it's the joy with which they can't play, happily lost in the moment, that's important.

Yep, even Bill and Ted are finding their flow.

So don't worry about whether you're 'Dave Beeth Oven' or not. Sometimes music should be more about catharsis than perfection, enjoying it simply as an emotional release. After all, confidence isn't 'They'll like me'. Confidence is 'I'll be fine if they don't'. Be brave enough to suck.

———

Keanu put this into practice in real life with his band Dogstar; friends bonded by punk and alt-rock. Keanu approached drummer Rob Mailhouse when he spotted him wearing a hockey shirt in a supermarket in the early nineties and they soon started jamming at the star's house under the Hollywood sign. 'We were more interested in the emotion of it, rather than actually listening to what we were doing at that particular time' remembers Mailhouse. Find the simplest truth like that and you will always be free; 'so absolutely free that your very existence is an act of rebellion', to quote legendary French thinker Albert Camus (sounding a lot like Morpheus from *The Matrix*).

It didn't matter that Dogstar went on to receive high-profile criticism, due to their bassist being Johnny Utah. It didn't matter that, during their show at the Glastonbury festival in 1999, Keanu was swatting away things being thrown at him like hockey pucks on the ice rink. The band simply laughed it off and 'put their faith in a loud guitar'.

'We just wanted
to play music and
that's what kept
us all together as
friends today.'

ROB MAILHOUSE, DOGSTAR

That's the rebellious joy of rock 'n' roll right there: *simplicity*. Three chords and the truth. 'We all just looked through the bullshit' admits Mailhouse. 'We just wanted to play music and that's what kept us all together as friends today'.

The simple drive needed to be in a band – indeed any kind of group – can be so satisfying, regardless of the obstacles in your way (or being hurled at you). It's the dream and the courage to be on top of the world that's important, more than any skill you might possess. Whether or not you actually 'make it' isn't the point. If you feel as if you have when you're playing, then you have.

It's those big dreams that give us a purpose in life and allows us to fight for what we believe in: the desire to be more than just another zombie caught in the Matrix or – even worse – just another average rock band without Eddie Van Halen on guitar.

——

Of course music doesn't have to be a deep statement. It can just be... well, *fun*. A hobby. Listening to it, playing it. Hobbies bring a sense of freedom to life that can help combat stress and exhaustion, a much needed work break that's something to look forward to after a hard day's saving the world. A sense of connection and purpose like that is one of the basic foundations for happiness.

Plus hobbies can provide a cheeky neurological workout too, especially being in a band. The simple act of playing an instrument requires different brain systems to work together, leading to a healthy change in brain activity. And that music certainly doesn't have to be complex either. In Keanu's case it's post-hardcore, street punk and thrash: 'Fugazi, the Ramones, Exploited, Discharge, early Elvis Costello, the Clash, Violent Femmes, Joy Division, Minor Threat, and Bad Brains. That's definitely what I cut my teeth on.'

If *that* can help you chill out, then anything can.

So who's in your band? Who are the people you can always rely on, that work in harmony with you? Even if you're not in an actual rock group, form an imaginary one by pinpointing the mates you can always count on. Solo artists are fine but even they need back-up. No one copes entirely alone. In fact, relationships have been shown to be as important to our physical health as eating well and keeping fit. Some reports have even concluded that having 'band mates' in our life fosters good brain health. Working in a group helps us to be each other's cheerleaders; to lift one another so that we can all be seen... and heard. **air guitar**

———

For Keanu at his happiest, check out the footage of him at the premiere of *Toy Story 4*, where he bumps into old friend – and Red Hot Chili Peppers' bassist – Flea.

'What's up, legend!' Keanu beams, no doubt recalling the time he and the man born Michael Balzary stayed in director Gus Van Sant's Portland home together during the filming of *My Own Private Idaho*.

The film-maker himself moved out, so hard was the partying.

You are who you surround yourself with and Keanu has frequently worked with rockers, from Faith No More's Jim Martin in *Bill & Ted's Bogus Journey* to Flea's Chili Peppers' bandmate Anthony Kiedis in *Point Break*. River Phoenix himself had a music career alongside his acting (often collaborating with another Chili Pepper, John Frusciante). Some of them took their playful attitude – one of the hallmarks of creativity – to tragically extreme lengths, yet there's an opposing perseverance that's key to creative people's success too. It's what makes them fascinating; often both extrovert *and* introvert, energetic *and* restful. *Psychology Today* christened it 'full blast living'.

Studies have shown creatives like that to be psychologically androgynous too, displaying not only the stereotypical strengths of their own gender (e.g. the compassionate female) but those of the other too (e.g. the risk-taking male). After all, you can't be truly creative and only think *inside* the box. Mostly though, creativity has been shown to induce happiness without any ulterior motive. That's its magic. It's about making something – be it music, movies or motorbikes – for the simple joy of making them.

'Being happy is a radical and desirable act if you ask me' Anthony Kiedis once said. And whilst Keanu might rarely smile, his demeanour suggests a similar contentment. Rockers can be rebellious and radical, of course. But they don't *have* to be angry.

———

You can't have rock 'n' roll rebellion without motorbikes. Keanu's future *Speed* co-star Dennis Hopper rode a Harley into the history books in counterculture classic *Easy Rider*; legendary sixties siren Marianne Faithful was naked under leathers in *Girl on a Motorcycle*; tiny Prince sat on his tiny Honda in *Purple Rain*...

Yet there's more to riding on two wheels than danger and daring; more than Duke Caboom doing jumps and crash landing. It can be meditative too. 'The agency that you have on a motorcycle is fantastic' Keanu reveals. 'A real kinda responsibility and connection. It's also the exposure to the elements. You can smell, hear, see in a different way on a motorcycle. The visceral experience of riding... I highly recommend it.'

You *have* to be mindful on a motorbike. If you're not in the zone you're likely on the side of the road. That hyper-awareness leads to a Zen-like flow, the miles just melting away beneath you. Plus, on a motorbike, even if you've got River Phoenix clinging to you, there's still an element of introspection. No talking, no distractions. 'Four wheels move the body, two wheels move the soul' goes the bikers' adage. Journalism bad boy – and fellow biker – Hunter S. Thompson put it more bluntly: 'Faster, faster, until the thrill of speed overcomes the fear of death'.

Riding at high speed – like surfing, skydiving and fighting – is the physical manifestation of the rock 'n' roll lifestyle: live fast, die young (although hopefully not). It's certainly a pastime that carries with it a huge amount of risk. Keanu himself has a false tooth as a result of a biking accident.

But what if there's a point to taking risks?

Through dabbling with danger we have to confront our own fears. Yes, sometimes that leads to mistakes that need a dentist – but it's the process of learning that's character building.

Thankfully it doesn't always have to involve a motorbike (that just depends on how rock 'n' roll you truly want to be). Taking *any* kind of risk forces us to face the fear of uncertainty and it's that process that's more useful than the actual outcome, helping us become more resilient and confident. It really is more about the journey than the destination – and who you might share that journey with.

'This girl was just the most rockin' girl in the world you could have on the back of a bike' Keanu reminisced about an ex back in 1989, 'because she was fuckin' fearless... we had no helmets and no goggles and we were going like a hundred and thirty miles an hour on five lanes of freeway, with not a soul in sight. And this incredible cloudless moon just hangin' there... I've had some of the best times of my life on a motorcycle'.

———

Keanu's lifestyle is less rockstar these days. He plays bass not quite so often, rides his Norton Commando a little slower, has fewer all-night parties. His system-smashing is now more virtual (playing punk activist Johnny Silverhand in video game 'Cyberpunk 2077') than actual. 'I guess it would have helped if our band was better' he told *GQ* in 2019, a little wistfully.

Yet the creative and collaborative power of music – from the lyrics to the lifestyle – has been therapy for him. Find your calling like that and it doesn't matter if you go at it full pelt or half speed. You'll have found your bliss.

'I've had some of the best times of my life on a motorcycle.' KEANU

#bemorekeanu tips for wannabe Wyld Stallyns:

1. *Don't worry if you suck.* Whatever your group – rock band or book club – happiness is in the journey not in some mythical idea of ultimate perfection.

2. *Find your bandmates.* Just as every instrument provides something crucial to a song – beat, rhythm, groove, melody – we rely on each other. Even loners like Keanu need back-up.

3. *Celebrate creativity.* Being creative can be wonderfully contradictory – strong and sensitive, happy and sad. Embrace that challenge.

4. *Risks aren't just rock 'n' roll.* They build character and help us learn. And they don't always have to involve haring around corners at sixty miles per hour.

5. *But mainly... enjoy yourself!* Being cool often comes with a sneer but the best way to stick it to the man is to be

unexpected. Passions are meant to be fun. Why be afraid to show it?

And, as Rufus reminds us in *Bogus Journey*, '... *do not* do your homework without wearing headphones!' That's one bit of multi-tasking even Keanu would recommend.

KEANU
THE
COMEDIAN

You know what's a better predictor of success than IQ?

EQ.

In the eighties EQ might have been a knob that you fiddled with on your hi-fi but these days it means Emotional Intelligence. In other words, how we understand ourselves and others. Can we control our emotions and help to manage other people's? Can we motivate ourselves and empathise with those struggling? And maybe most importantly, do we know our own strengths and weaknesses? Are we self-aware?

A Harvard Business Review study revealed the most confident and focused leaders are exactly that: wholly aware of their personalities. And the best way to spot self-awareness like that is by looking for a self-deprecating sense of humour. After all, people that can admit to their shortcomings, who don't take themselves too seriously, are approachable because they're in on the joke. They know what we know. It's transparency at its most harmonising, at its most entertaining.

And that's Keanu in *Toy Story 4*.

Not only does he throw in a trademark 'Whoa!' as a verbal wink, Duke Caboom himself is all too aware of the difference between image and reality. As a toy he's sold as 'Canada's greatest stuntman', macho and moustachioed, an acrobat on two wheels. As a man he's had to deal with the disappointing truth that he can't live up to his own advertising. It's Keanu letting us know that, as badass as he might be on film, real life is never quite so easy. It's the clash that's funny. And it makes us love him all the more.

'Humour is the great thing' wrote Mark Twain. 'The minute it crops up, all our hardnesses yield, all our irritations, and resentments flit away, and a sunny spirit takes their place'. Sounds like he would have loved *Bill & Ted*.

—

Keanu's cameo in Netflix's rom-com *Always Be My Maybe* went even further. Playing a version of himself – this one rocking pseudo-intellectual glasses – he sent-up his guru status by wheeling out zingers such as 'The only stars that matter are the ones you look at when you dream' and claiming Mother Teresa as his childhood crush. Well, it makes a change from Jessica Rabbit I guess.

Such self-deprecation wasn't hard for him. 'We were talking about the character, and he just had so many funny ideas and pitches that we went back and revised the script with those in mind' said director Nahnatchka Khan. Keanu then followed *that* internet-breaking cameo with another: in *The Spongebob Movie: Sponge on the Run*, playing a sage... made of actual sage.

Science has made it clear: 90 percent of men and 81 percent of women report that a sense of humour is the most important quality in a partner. 'If you are making a woman laugh' Keanu once whispered, 'you are seeing the most beautiful thing on God's Earth'.

Returning with *Bill & Ted Face the Music*, now as an adult, shows that Keanu still relishes those laughs. He wouldn't have signed on to briefly voice the title character – a cat (yes, *a cat*) – in Jordan Peele's 2016's buddy comedy *Keanu* if he didn't.

Silliness like that makes the hard times easier to survive, encourages us to question why we take everything so seriously and get stressed. Some – like Ted's dad – might disagree, thinking that silliness should be left to little children, that it's something we should grow out of. Perhaps, though, silliness is one of the most mature things we can give to the world? After all, it carries with it no fear, violence or suffering. Playing silly erases vanity and ego. The world could do with more of that.

—

'If you are making
a woman laugh you
are seeing the most
beautiful thing on
God's Earth.'

KEANU

—

Keanu has long been nonplussed by the world of ego. 'The idea [of fame]... is so abstract. It's really cool to have a response to what you've done, but it's not something I like to search out in my spare time' he said in 1989.

Thankfully that spare time is filled with much more worthwhile pursuits like riding motorbikes, reading books... and having a laugh.

———

Oddly, many Ancient Greek and Early Christian thinkers were surprisingly sniffy about laughter. It was someone out of control, they complained, or feeling superior over another. It's why seeing straight-faced Socrates interact with bonkers Bill and Ted is so funny.

Now studies can see comedy's benefit. Jokes can foster a tolerance for diversity, build trust and reduce conflict. They can be blind to class and education too, proving even slackers like Bill and Ted to be inspirational. In communicating tough news, a lightness of mood can smoothly reduce negative emotions. Just look at Keanu using quips to deflect from talking about his private life in interviews. He could get annoyed. Instead he gets jokey.

And there are even physical benefits.

STICK ON *BOGUS JOURNEY* AND ENJOY THE FOLLOWING GIFTS:

1. *Laughter relaxes.* A belly laugh relieves tension and stress, leaving your muscles relaxed for up to 45 minutes after. *No way? Yes way!*

2. *Laughter boosts the immune system.* Chuckle your way to fewer stress hormones and more immune cells and infection-fighting antibodies. The result? A better resistance to infection. *Excellent!*

3. *Laughter gets you buzzing.* It's all about

the endorphins produced, your feel-good chemicals. Not only do they help with an overall sense of well-being, they can even temporarily help with pain. *Whoa!*

4. *Laughter protects the heart.* Giggles improve the functioning of blood vessels and boost blood flow, helping to protect against heart problems. *Most non-heinous!*

5. *Laughter is slimming (sort of).* 'Reaping burns a lot of calories' according to Death in *Bogus Journey* but it's a lot more fun to simply have a good chuckle. Ten to fifteen minutes a day can burn approximately forty calories. *Get down with your bad self!*

—

Critics haven't always been kind about Keanu's acting ('it often seems as if he's reading from cue cards rather than saying words that are his' wrote one) but as someone who's happy to mix those comedy roles with thrillers, dramas, sci-fi and romance, he's shown a range few others could entertain.

'A good bad actor' some have more generously called him and at least, when he sends himself up, Keanu shows us he knows it too. Who cares that he's more of a presence than a true thespian? No-one's claiming he's Daniel Day-Lewis. Crucially, he's prepared to go with that, working the comedy muscles as much as any of the others. After all, it's not enough to be strong if you lack endurance. It's not enough to be fast if you lack power. The person who is well-rounded is so often the person who excels; the person with a high EQ.

Plus, Daniel Day-Lewis would suck in Wyld Stallyns.

Being more Keanu means welcoming variety, whatever people say about your versatility. Criticisms don't control us, we control them. We can choose if we want them to play a part in our life or not. Keanu's had more than his fair share of criticism but refuses to let it affect him. 'I get negative shit all the time' he admits. And the way to handle it? 'I don't care'.

Keanu's earliest successes were in comedy: *Parenthood*, *I Love You to Death*, the *Bill & Teds*. Lighter, goofier roles were what he became famous for. Luckily, though, he didn't let his past define his future. He used our preconception of him as a joker to change things up, defying expectations with his choices. Smart move.

What we did in the last month, last year, even in childhood, shouldn't deny us the chance of reinvention like that. Of course real change is often painful, otherwise it's likely you're not changing enough, and Keanu's move from comedy to drama was perhaps especially painful for critics who thought they had him all figured out.

145

But it's all about *emodiversity* – i.e. displaying a broad range of emotions in a balanced way. Be true to how you are feeling at a certain time, your authentic mood, and your wellbeing will thank you for it. After the tragic early death of his friend River Phoenix, Keanu wanted to be – *needed* to be – serious for a while. After all, how satisfying would simple repetition be? Choosing courage over comfort widened his horizons and, in turn, ultimately improved our opinion of him. Even the critics were won over (eventually).

—

'I get negative shit all the time. I don't care.'

KEANU

Don't worry that being committed to core values means being stuck in your ways, either. It's actually quite the contrary. Keanu makes himself *flexible* to ensure he remains true to himself. He wasn't the one being stubborn over not wanting to make *Speed 2*. Rather it was the film company who were steadfast, determined to be unimaginative in predictably making a sequel. Keanu just moved on and stayed authentic, playing with his band instead of starring in a supposed high-velocity action movie that was set on... a slow-moving cruise liner. Eight Golden Raspberry nominations later and Keanu had the last laugh.

So it's all about knowing your 'why'; determining your mission, what underpins your sense of integrity. Work that out and you'll instinctively understand when to try something new and when to say 'no'. The key to greatness in any walk of life – to influence and longevity – is that sense of unwavering character and purpose. And that can bend to work in any situation.

So what's your 'why'?

For Keanu, it's all about variety and authenticity; a self-awareness of when to play the joker, when to play the hero... and when to play the bass.

And that's a whole lot healthier than just being a great actor.

———

#bemorekeanu tips for using laughter in your life:

1. *Chuckle at yourself.* Giggle at your shortcomings. Transparency like that is mentally beneficial – and, let's be honest, just plain attractive.
2. *Embrace the silly.* It's good for your body – all those endorphins! – and good for the world.
3. *Laugh... and cry.* Variety works wonders for your emotional wellbeing... and in proving the critics wrong.

4. *Be flexible.* It's crucial to know your mission statement but being true to yourself means moving too. Others stay still. You make daredevil jumps.

Altogether now:

'Let's caboom!'

KEANU
THE
LOVER

Keanu is too Zen to be a player. Even when he plays a bad boy – as in 2001's rom-com *Sweet November* – the story is about him realising the error of his ways. The guy can't stay that way for long. He's manly, yes – but too caring to be boringly macho.

That blend has a powerful effect on several movie characters: they're *desperate* to seduce him. From *Dracula*'s lusty brides to the playful girls in *Knock Knock*; from the five daughters of the demon Mara in *Little Buddha*... to Bodhi in *Point Break*. They can't get enough. Poor Keanu's so shocked his hair goes grey because of the first, gets tied up with a hose and buried in the garden after the second, eradicates his ego in the third and deliberately misfires his load (of bullets) after the fourth.

All he really wanted to do was just get on with his work.

It's that conviction that keeps Keanu's roles sexy but not calculated. He doesn't *try* to be attractive. He's too dedicated to stopping the bus, to finding the mainframe, to avenging Daisy's death. 'Get your hands off my wife!' he growls at Gary Oldman's deliciously sleazy Dracula, entirely committed to his other half (Winona Ryder). In the patchy *Replicas* he even tries to resurrect his late partner by using his scientific knowledge of 'Neurofibrillary tangles' (spoiler: it's not a good idea). The point is, he's an earnest and devoted partner. And that makes him hot.

There's an old Buddhist proverb that says: 'When walking, walk. When eating, eat'.

Purity equals conviction and conviction equals confidence. And confidence is sexy. Keanu's co-star in *The Matrix*, Carrie-Anne Moss, certainly saw it: 'He's Zen-like... He's incredibly focused and incredibly disciplined, and I mean unlike anyone I've ever met'.

As Danceny, the music teacher in *Dangerous Liaisons*, Keanu's not part of the upper class set who require his services. He's better than them though. When he goes to the opera it's to weep at the emotion of the music, to be lost in the moment, not to just socialise and show off. John Malkovich's Valmont is the opposite – cold, deliberate, preening – but Danceny is entirely caught up in the passion of it all. It's that conviction again. No wonder Uma Thurman and Glenn Close want a piece of his purity.

Meanwhile in the world of *The Matrix Reloaded*, Neo has rampant rave music sex with Trinity to help her feel grounded, then snogs Persephone to make her feel more than just a computer program. Women crave his pure intensity to remind them what raw feelings are. *Awesome!*

'The simple act of paying attention can take you a long way' Keanu once said. It's true. Nothing is as much of a turn-on as attention. As a lovestruck Annie mumbles to Jack after a death-defying day in *Speed*: 'You didn't leave me'.

HOW TO BE MORE ATTENTIVE WHEN SOMEONE IS SPEAKING:

1. *Maintain eye contact.* It shows attention. It's not a staring competition though. That would just be creepy. Relax.

2. *Try not to judge.* Don't jump to conclusions before the speaker has finished. Interruptions = turn-off.

3. *Look for non-verbal cues too.* How is the speaker's tone of voice, their body

language? Are they communicating more than they're saying?

4. *Don't give advice.* Solutions are best only when they're asked for. Keanu would never mansplain.

'The simple act of paying attention can take you a long way.' KEANU

That attention has wooed Sandra Bullock not once but twice: first of all in that rom-com-with-bombs, *Speed*, then in 2006's *The Lake House* (the time-travelling letterbox movie you never knew you needed). Really, Sandy is Keanu's perfect movie partner – another casually sexy deity; discrete in private and often a loner in films too, yet with the banter to warm even Keanu's cold cockles. The rumours are they crushed on each other back in the day, just never acted on it – a missed opportunity that has only made us love them all the more.

The Lake House couldn't have been more different to *Speed*. Telling the gently fantastical story of two people falling in love through letters, though strangely separated by two years (don't ask), it's a hymn to self-restraint and commitment. Perhaps it should have been called *Slow*?

Riffing on Jane Austen's *Persuasion* (a book 'about waiting', Bullock's character Kate helpfully explains), *The Lake House* is the overlooked noughties romance that now – in an era where we're all urged to slow down, switch off and be mindful – takes on a new pertinence. It's cheesy, of course, but Keanu gives it his usual blend of the everyday and the enigmatic – the most ethereal pick-up truck driver you're ever likely to meet. The two leads hold out for each and that's the point. Romance doesn't have to be quick; it is probably better when it isn't. True love waits.

The loss of slowness – of quiet contemplation, solitude, silence, focusing on one thing at a time – is a relatively recent change in society that we never seemed to have a say on. Did we miss the meeting? Even dating is now an instant swipe right. Technology has accelerated so quickly – Google is less than thirty years old – that we haven't properly allowed ourselves to work out how it affects our relationships. Yet with every carefully thought-out answer and every languidly delivered line of dialogue – plus that distinct lack of social media – Keanu's life is one of old-fashioned prudence and self-control.

So maybe try slowing down too? During the enforced lockdown for Covid-19 many psychologists championed the idea of 'post traumatic growth' – i.e. trying to learn from the shock new pace of life we had to adopt. Why? Because slowness makes you realise who and what are truly important to you. It has a beautiful way of sifting the wheat from the chaff, the Bullocks from the bollocks.

———

When Keanu went public with girlfriend Alexandra Grant at a Los Angeles County Museum of Art event in 2019, it was the first time he'd been open about a relationship in twenty years. The press went crazy. After all, she was *nearly* his own age (actually nine years younger but that's close enough for Hollywood).

Yet anyone who's watched Keanu in *Something's Gotta Give* – where his character Julian dates Diane Keaton's Erica, twenty years his senior – knows that age (rightfully) means nothing to him. He and Diane were even rumoured to have dated in real life. They were certainly more than happy to flirt together again as presenters at the 2020 Oscars – so much so that *Something's Gotta Give* writer/director Nancy Myers wondered on Twitter if their characters should have actually ended up together in the film. 'When something happens to you that hasn't happened before, don't you at least have to find out what it is?' asks Julian – and of course he's right. Investigate emotions not numbers. If you don't make an issue of age, age isn't an issue.

It's the same with gender. Exhibit one: *Point Break*. Exhibit two: *My Own Private Idaho*. Exhibit three: when Keanu was rumoured to have been having a relationship with media mogul David Geffen in the nineties he didn't get angry. He actually said he was flattered, since Geffen was a very dashing man.

It's that openness that has made Keanu an icon for all sexualities. And one of the best things about an open mind like that is the vulnerability that comes with it. In enjoying a liberal view of the world, you're basically admitting to not knowing everything, that there are new things out there to experience. And that's exhilarating in both work and love. As Charlize Theron's bewitching Sara tells Keanu's Nelson in *Sweet November*: 'You don't have to understand me. You just need to let it happen'.

Ah, *Sweet November*. Uptight rich boy meets crazy boho girl and they fall in love. Cute story, right?

Yet – and apologies for bursting bubbles here – unlikely. Although it's simple looks that initially attract us to someone (and Keanu and Charlize have few problems in that department), research shows that it's actually common backgrounds which keep a relationship together; education, work, politics etc. If you do buck the trend and fall for someone with a completely different outlook on life to you, great. But you're also more likely to get into arguments later.

That's not to entirely discount the plot of *Sweet November* or indeed a film such as 2018's *Destination Wedding* – a movie where bickering strangers Frank (Keanu) and Lindsay (Winona Ryder) meet during a marriage weekend and, after initially not liking each other... well, you can guess the rest. A little room for manoeuvre in a relationship is a good thing. Find someone that's your immediate perfect fit and where's the space for growing, learning and moving forward?

Plus, it's Keanu and Winona. *Of course* they'll end up liking each other.

Ultimately, though, relationships need deep similarities to steady the surface differences. A building with strong foundations can take a few cracks in the ceiling.

—

'Because we're actors we can pretend and fake it but I'd rather the intimate investment was authentic.' KEANU

All of which destroys the myth of a lot of Hollywood rom-coms. We might like to *believe* that opposites attract but the numbers just don't back it up. Really, we just don't want a partner who completely challenges our world view or that we have to pretend to agree with. Validation and honesty feels much better than the anger of disagreement or the charade of lying. 'Because we're actors we can pretend and fake it' admits Keanu, 'but I'd rather the intimate investment was authentic'. Sensible man.

Keanu's partner Alexandra Grant was, like him, the child of a broken marriage and – also like him – brought up by her mother in a variety of locations around the world. Today she is a visual artist who creates work influenced by language and linguistics. She's even collaborated with Keanu himself on a couple of occasions. The couple share strong foundations. Both like to question the role of humanity in today's technology-fuelled world – whether that's Alex turning textual images into visual forms and exploring notions of translation and identity through the media of painting, photography and sculpture... or Keanu kicking ass in *The Matrix*.

———

Keanu's love life hit the tabloids when tragedy struck in the early noughties but has still largely been kept out of the press. That's no fluke. Despite rumours of romance with other film types – Sofia Coppola, Parker Posey, Claire Forlani – he has never sought publicity for his relationships. For years, he didn't even seem to have any. 'My private life is a boring disaster' he said in 2008, either revealing the truth or cunningly throwing reporters off the scent.

When it comes to wellbeing, that kind of modesty makes sense. Giving too much away is often a sign of insecurity, feeling that you can only get recognition and love if you offer something of yourself. Unfortunately that leads to everyone feeling like they own you. And from *that* comes paranoia.

Being quieter about those things closest to you, on the other hand, means that the ones who *genuinely* share your life – friends, family – get more of you. There's a deeper, more profound understanding. They trust you. Even gossip-mongers, for their part, learn to stay away.

And where would Keanu be without that sense of mystery? It sets up a challenge: get to know me properly and maybe I'll let you in. A quiet depth like that indicates reliability. He knows his values and his preferences and he'll stick to them, certainly not swayed by fashions or fads. 'I live for one thing: to love you, to make you happy, to live firmly and joyously in the moment' promises Nelson in *Sweet November*.

Who wants an attention seeker when you can have an attention *giver*.

'I live for one thing: to love you, to make you happy, to live firmly and joyously in the moment.'

NELSON MOSS, *SWEET NOVEMBER*

#bemorekeanu tips for a most righteous romance:

1. *Pay attention.* Listening to someone is caring. And caring is – how should we put it? – *hot.*

2. *Take time.* Nature doesn't hurry yet still gets everything done. Why not try the same with finding Mr/Ms/Mx Right?

3. *Be vulnerable.* Admit you don't know everything about love and unexpected doors will open up.

4. *Look for core similarities.* Opposites attract but don't always last. Similar backgrounds, attitudes, or opinions on *The Matrix* franchise make for strong foundations.

5. *Keep something back.* Spotlights are great for a film set, not so great for trusting relationships.

'I'm Mickey Mouse' Keanu once quipped.
'They don't know who's inside the suit'.
It's a commitment to privacy that makes
sense. By only taking off those red shorts
and massive yellow shoes for your loved
ones, you build a bond of authenticity that
can never be broken.

KEANU

THE

PIONEER

Back in the late eighties, it wasn't just that we'd never *heard* the name Keanu before. The fact that it also meant something intangible, meditative – that Hawaiian 'cool breeze' – made him extra special and exotic. Tom Cruise couldn't match *that*.

And while his name put Keanu's Polynesian heritage front and centre of his stardom, it's the man as a mix that's been most exciting. In an industry that tries to pigeonhole, Keanu has always celebrated (modestly, of course) his own diversity. The first producers he met in Hollywood wanted him to change his name to the more predictable 'KC Reeves'. The man himself even considered (wait for it) Chuck Spadina and Templeton Taylor.

'It's so not who I am' he told *Rolling Stone* magazine later. 'Other people say, "If you want to do what you want to do, you have to do this." And the lesson being – you know what? You don't. You don't.'

Yep. Keanu Reeves was a wise old man by the time he was twenty.

———

'Every struggle in your life has shaped you into the person you are today.'

KEANU

Keanu's childhood was one of wandering – from Beirut to Sydney, New York to Toronto. What would be anomalistic to some was his norm and it helped make him the free spirit that he is. Reeves's mother, Patricia, was a former dancer who designed costumes for musicians and his father – more errant, a drug user – left them when Keanu was still a toddler. Of course it had an impact ('The story with me and my dad's pretty heavy. It's full of pain and woe and fucking loss and all that shit') but Keanu and his contemporaries – River, Winona, Uma – all used their bohemian backgrounds to quickly establish their range in the burgeoning indie cinema world. Their childhood eccentricities and sensitivities were celebrated, not glossed over.

The lesson? Let your individuality shine. If you're one of the crowd, staying in your comfort zone, no one's going to notice you. Be true to your unique history though and you'll find your special place. Everyone has something waiting to be expressed. Every life has a purpose. 'Every struggle in your life' believes Keanu, 'has shaped you into the person you are today'.

—

Those struggles resulted in some pioneering roles; at the forefront of the grunge and slacker movements with *River's Edge*, a trailblazer of Queer Cinema with *My Own Private Idaho*. The latter's director Gus Van Sant came straight out of Portland, a low-budget and radically un-Hollywood film-maker crafting idiosyncratic and strange tales of drifters and rootlessness. 1991 Keanu – hot from *Bogus Journey* and *Point Break* – could have signed on to multiple mainstream blockbusters if he'd been so inclined.

Instead he chose Van Sant's story of two Oregon rent boys. 'Keanu's on a movie star track' *Idaho's* producer Laurie Parker told *Elle* magazine that year, '... but he has a hell-bent streak; he's up for doing something free.' Hell-bent or heaven-sent?

'To be yourself in a world that is constantly trying to make you something else is the greatest accomplishment' wrote nineteenth-century American thinker Ralph Waldo Emerson.

There's another dude who totally knows how to #bemorekeanu.

MOVIES THAT KEANU HAS TURNED DOWN (AND THE REASON WHY):

1. *Platoon* (1986). He didn't like the violence.

2. *The Fly II* (1989). He didn't like the dodgy script.

3. *Heat* (1995). He wanted to play Hamlet on stage in Canada instead.

4. *Watchmen* (2009). 'It didn't work out' says Keanu.

5. *Captain Marvel* (2019). He was busy kicking ass making *John Wick: Chapter 3*.

'Other people say, "If you want to do what you want to do, you have to do this." And the lesson being – you know what? You don't. You don't.'

KEANU

As the eighties morphed into the nineties – during the worst of the AIDS crisis and with the morals of the LGBT community still questioned by the mainstream – playing gay hadn't yet become the thing for actors to do, not even for the new wave of boho slackers. Making a film like *My Own Private Idaho*, essentially a meditation on gay male desire, at a time when Hollywood really wasn't used to tackling that, was the ultimate expression of creative freedom.

'I was introduced to so many elements through the guy I was playing' Keanu told *Interview* magazine. 'Real people. My imagination. Gus's interpretation. Shakespeare. It was rich! And it was just bottomless, man. You could go as far as you could go, you know?'

Yet Keanu had shown his allegiance to queer culture even earlier. In 1984, as an unknown in Toronto, he'd starred in a local play called *Wolfboy* – a gay romance between two troubled teenage boys.

'He was a knockout. There was an honesty about him' remembers director John Palmer. 'He had so much energy that he didn't know what to do with.'

Restlessness like that might never disappear but at least it can be channelled elsewhere; the adrenaline that comes with anxiety transformed into something productive rather than simply being muted. 'Energy can't be created or destroyed, and energy flows' says Keanu, displaying his knowledge of The First Law of Thermodynamics (naturally). 'It must be in... some kind of internal, emotive, spiritual direction. It must have some effect somewhere'.

We have all been given the power to create positive experiences through our choices, but if we believe that *other* forces rule how we live then we give away all that power. Pioneering means going out on a limb, standing by our decisions. Do we really have control over our life unless we are willing to take responsibility for it?

If such decisions saw Keanu become an icon of contemporary nineties disillusionment he was quick to change that up too. Did he say 'no' to playing Jonathan Harker in *Bram Stoker's Dracula* because he didn't think he *could* play a staid nineteenth-century clerk in a law firm? Of course not. He signed up. The fact that he was, well, kinda terrible doesn't matter. (Sample dialogue: 'We can be mawwied when I weturn'.) At least he kept himself intrigued and us on our toes. Someone that restless would never allow themselves to be pigeonholed.

———

Speed was loud and explosive, the film that fully confirmed former indie kid Keanu as a kick-ass tough guy (who still looked cool with most of his hair cut off). It was quietly pioneering too. The majority of the action took place on a Santa Monica bus, the supporting cast of passengers a mix of races and backgrounds, all of whom Keanu's Jack is desperate to save (and Sandra Bullock's Annie appears to be friends with). It's multiculturalism on four wheels. The bad guy – Dennis Hopper – is white. The good guy – Jack – is... well, who knows? We find out nothing about Jack's life or his heritage. He's just a blank page in a tight white t-shirt, a hero to all with no specific roots to colour our feelings.

Keanu frequently broke new ground back then in choosing roles that played up to his own individual ethnicities – Chinese, Hawaiian, Canadian, American, British – yet also sometimes, as in *Speed*, finding something that championed the blend of them too. The unique result offered a hero for almost everyone. And symbols of harmony like that matter. After all, if we can't *see* what we can be, we can't be it.

In the vivid 2006 adaptation of Philip K. Dick's sci-fi *A Scanner Darkly*, Keanu plays Bob, an undercover agent wearing a so-called 'scramble suit' that changes his exterior into what's described as a 'constantly shifting vague blur'. He's literally anyone and everyone. Meanwhile as the hero to a multi-racial resistance in *The Matrix*, the unifying Neo offers the chance of 'a world without rules and controls, without borders or boundaries. A world where anything is possible'.

It's Keanu's very ambiguity that changes our perspective of what can be achieved.

After all, if he can be whatever we want
him to be, the possibilities are endless. So
honour your own stories and cherish them
but don't hold anything too tightly. 'Multi-
culture is the real culture of the world –
a pure race doesn't exist' Keanu reminds
us. His own background proves it.
Okay, Agent Smith in *The Matrix* might
call a world like that 'a zoo' but he's a
computer program, a heartless conformer.
Neo, on the other hand, is all about the
beauty of free will; a pioneer in the prison
of the Matrix. Neo wouldn't build a wall.
He'd have a party.

––––

Poor Will Smith. When he was offered the chance to play Neo in *The Matrix*, he turned it down. Big Willy, it seems, didn't have a Big Imagination. He just couldn't see how the film would succeed. Keanu, on the other hand, sensed something special.

'It is incredibly empowering to know that your future is in your hands' Keanu has reminded us, but it's a remarkable level of intuition – not *just* his hands – that has helped him to shape his future. As someone who'd been making intriguing choices for ten years prior to *The Matrix*, Keanu's gut instinct was well-honed when it came to joining the groundbreaking post-apocalyptic sci-fi. He found a film that perfectly chimed with pre-millennial tension, the rise of VR and the boom in Nu-Metal; a myth for the digital age that mixed philosophy and fighting like never before and even sold itself on its Asian-tinged, brainbox qualities. This wasn't just a film. It was a rallying cry for outsiders everywhere, a command to 'Be a little more you and a lot less them' in movie form. Will Smith couldn't quite claim the same for *Wild Wild West*.

'I loved the material when I first read it' Keanu's admitted, 'and the experience of making [*The Matrix*] was a great one. So when we came around to complete the trilogy, I just signed on board without even reading the scripts because the experience of the first film was so good.'

It's an instinct that hasn't gone away either. Loving the potential of *John Wick*, Keanu signed up quickly – presumably before Will Smith had a chance.

———

Being a pioneer means not being afraid of difficult questions and one of Keanu's favourites is a major headscratcher:

What is real?

No other actor has welcomed that most

postmodern of conundrums into Western films in quite the same way (it crops up in movies such as *Johnny Mnemonic*, *The Matrix*, *Bogus Journey* and *A Scanner Darkly*). In *The Day the Earth Stood Still* – kind of a *Close Encounters of the Keanu Kind* – he makes clear, as an alien life form clad in a human's skin, that all is not what it seems: 'This body will take some getting used to'.

That separation of mind and body is something thinkers as far back as René Descartes in the seventeenth century have been pondering, but in today's world of digital manipulation it has extra pertinence. The world of *The Matrix* was a 'deep fake' before we even knew what the term meant. Jean Baudrillard tackled this modern-day issue of copy and imitation head on in 1983 with his seminal book *Simulacra and Simulation*. No surprise, then, that Neo's got a copy on his bookshelf.

And no surprise either that bookworm Keanu read it all before filming.

———

The biggest film of 1999 – the year of *The Matrix* – was actually *Star Wars Episode 1: The Phantom Menace*, a movie where kiddy-friendly 'rasta' alien Jar Jar Binks says things like 'Icky, icky goo!' Yet all these years later, no-one's asking us to #bemorejarjar.

Why? Because authenticity ages so much better than the quick cash-in. Over the years, and in films of all tones, Keanu has played roles that encourage both a healthy scepticism and a rigorous intellect – an honest reflection of who he is. Not every movie has been a success at the box office or with critics but that's not always a guarantee of longevity anyway. Truly pioneering spirits are what stay the course.

And whilst it's increasingly unusual for Hollywood to revel in the grey areas and ask those big, complex questions, it's hugely important that they do. After all, it's only through tackling difficult problems that we broaden our understanding. It's only through looking inwards that we learn to not just #bemorekeanu but also to be the most important person of all: *ourselves*.

——

#bemorekeanu tips to help you push the boundaries:

1. *Be open to new experiences.* Seeking novelty doesn't have to mean doing crazy things. It just means doing fresh things.

2. *Stimulate your mind.* No one ever pioneered anything in the comfort zone.

3. *Be creative.* Slavishly memorising stuff is one thing but it's kinda boring. Allow your brain to think creatively and you're more likely to stay with a challenge and find something new.

4. *Avoid the shortcut. The Matrix* films aren't classics because they went for the lowest common denominator.

They're happily cerebral, refusing easy answers.

5. *Talk.* Even Keanu talks. Okay, maybe not a whole bunch but he talks to the right people: fellow pioneers. And then, suitably inspired, it's down to him to move forward.

'Teachers open the doors. You enter by yourself' goes the old Chinese proverb. Morpheus said it even better: 'I'm trying to free your mind, Neo. But I can only show you the door. You're the one that has to walk through it'.

So now you know how to #bemorekeanu, it's time to set off on *your* most triumphant journey.

Enjoy the ride, dudes!

ABOUT THE AUTHOR

James King is a writer, broadcaster and film critic who appears regularly on radio and television. He is also a qualified fitness instructor and longtime yoga student. His favourite Keanu film is *My Own Private Idaho* although he is also more than happy to defend *The Lake House*.

1 3 5 7 9 10 8 6 4 2

Square Peg, an imprint of Vintage,
20 Vauxhall Bridge Road,
London SW1V 2SA

Square Peg is part of the Penguin Random House group
of companies whose addresses can be found at
global.penguinrandomhouse.com

Text copyright © James King 2020
Illustrations copyright © Kate Holderness 2020

James King has asserted his right to be identified as the
author of this Work in accordance with the Copyright,
Designs and Patents Act 1988

First published by Square Peg in 2020

Penguin.co.uk/vintage

A CIP catalogue record for this book is available from
the British Library

ISBN 9781529110326

Typeset and designed by Anna Green

Printed and bound in Great Britain by Clays Ltd, Elcograf S.p.A.

Penguin Random House is committed to a sustainable future
for our business, our readers and our planet. This book is
made from Forest Stewardship Council® certified paper.